F-14
Tomcat

F-14
Tomcat
Tony Holmes

OSPREY
AEROSPACE

Published in 1990 by Osprey Publishing
Limited
59 Grosvenor Street, London W1X 9DA

British Library Cataloguing in Publication
Data

Holmes. Tony
    F-14 Tomcat.
    1. United States. Navy. Fighter
    aeroplanes, history
    I. Title II. Series
    623.74640973

ISBN 1-85532-126-2

Designed by Paul Kime
Printed in Hong Kong

Front cover Twin turbofans screeching as
the pilot tweaks the throttles to maintain
the correct approach angle to the carrier, a
subdued Tomcat from VF-111 'Sundowners'
closes on the ramp of USS *Carl Vinson*
(CVN-70). Embarked on the '*Vinson* in
November 1985 as part of Carrier Air Wing
(CVW) 15's carrier qualification period, this
particular Tomcat flew many 'bump and
burn' sorties with various 'Sundowner'
crews during the squadron's two-week
period at sea (*Frank B Mormillo*)

Back cover Partaking in a spot of intra-
squadron dogfighting, a pair of VF-302
'Superheats' F-14As 'mix it' out over the
Gulf of Mexico. Along with fellow reservists
VF-301 'Rangers', the 'Superheats' fly out of
NAS Dallas, Texas, as part of the east coast
reserve air wing, CVWR-20 (*Zone Five*)

Title page Hulking down the starboard side
of the USS *Carl Vinson* (CVN-70), this
blotchy F-14A belongs to VF-111. Although
hidden from this angle, a garish setting sun
motif adorns each of the twin fins on this
aircraft. A close inspection of the cockpit,
however, reveals that both the pilot and his
RIO are proudly 'flying' VF-111 colours on
their bonedomes (*Frank B Mormillo*)

Half title page Although technically not the
best photograph in this volume, this classic
shot, taken aboard USS *Forrestal* (CV-59) in
1971, is of major importance nevertheless.
Ranged up on bow cat one is the tenth pre-
production series F-14, BuNo 157989.
Playing its part in clearing the Tomcat for
frontline service, this appropriately marked
prototype piled up the launches and traps
during its fleeting stay aboard ship. Parked
on the bow are two CVW-17 A-6A
Intruders from VA-65, whilst the garishly
coloured F-4J belongs to the Navy Test
Directorate at Naval Air Test Center
Patuxent River, Maryland, the Phantom II
serving as a chase-plane for the Tomcat
whilst it was embarked on the *Forrestal*.
Returning to Pax River soon after this
photo was taken, this F-14 later earned the
rather unfortunate distinction of being the
second Tomcat written-off when it crashed
in Chesapeake Bay on 30 June 1972 during
rehearsals for an airshow at the test center
(*US Navy via David Brown*)

Contents

Right Perhaps the most famous of all naval fighter squadron emblems, 'Felix and the bomb' have been associated with VF-31 'Tomcatters' since the early 1930s. This blotchy fin is attached to the Commander Air Group's (CAG) F-14, parked aboard USS *Forrestal* (CV-59). Unlike most squadrons, VF-31 spray their aircraft up so the two-letter tailcode (in this case, 'AE') is on the inside of the F-14's twin fins (*Yves Debay*)

Go West
Young Grumman

Continental USA is pock-marked with military airfields both large and small, some being home to just a single Air National Guard unit, whilst others are overflowing with 'star-spangled' heavy metal. Most definitely in the latter category, the sprawling facility at Naval Air Station (NAS) Miramar is perhaps the most famous of them all, 'Fightertown USA' being known around the globe as the home of 'Top Gun'. An intergral part of the US Navy since the early 1950s, NAS Miramar owes its notoriety to one aircraft, and one aircraft alone – the stylish Grumman F-14 Tomcat.

No less than 13 fighter squadrons roost at Miramar, the base overflowing with Tomcats all year round. A common sight in the blue skies of southern California, the swing-wing Grumman fighter has darkened Miramar's ramp with its distinctive shape since October 1972. At that time the F-4 Phantom II was the battle seasoned veteran of the base, the west coast fighter community having taken the war to Hanoi for seven years. Now, the unrivalled supremacy of the 'St Louis Slugger' was under threat from a youthful product from Calverton, New York. Eventually, over the next 12 years, the F-4 would be totally replaced in fleet service by the F-14, the Tomcat deploying to sea on all Pacific fleet carriers, bar the small USS *Midway* (CV-41), on WestPac deployments.

Whether patrolling the warm waters of the Persian Gulf, covering the evacuation of Saigon during operation 'Frequent Wind', or just performing 'bump and burns' during practice deck landings at Miramar, the Tomcat has never been found wanting by its crews. Now a new breed of F-14 is appearing in the San Diego skies. Powered by new engines and having its avionics drastically upgraded, both the F-14A+(Plus) and the F-14D are well equipped to keep US Navy crews at the cutting edge of their profession well into the 21st century. The Tomcat has been an important asset in the Navy's arsenal for almost 20 years now, but it's not totally unreasonable to suggest that pilots and RIOs could find themselves walking out onto the sundrenched flight line at Miramar and strapping aboard a veteran F-14 in 20 years' time.

F-14 Tomcat Squadrons at NAS Miramar

VF-1	'Wolfpack'	VF-124	'Gunfighters'
VF-2	'Bounty Hunters'	VF-154	'Black Knights'
VF-21	'Freelancers'	VF-211	'Fighting Checkmates'
VF-24	'Fighting Renegades'	VF-213	'Black Lions'
VF-51	'Screaming Eagles'	VF-301	'Devil's Disciples'
VF-111	'Sundowners'	VF-302	'Stallions'
VF-114	'Aardvarks'		

Previous pages With its hook visible just below the tyre on the starboard gear leg, this Tomcat of VF-1 'Wolfpack' looks like it may jag a two-wire as it comes back aboard USS *Ranger* (CV-61). Toting a live AIM-9L Sidewinder on the wing shoulder pylon, and an AIM-54B Phoenix beneath the fuselage, this F-14 is in the throws of completing yet another combat air patrol (CAP) during *Ranger's* 'mini' WestPac in support of exercise *Team Spirit* '87 off the coast of South Korea (*Tony Holmes*)

Above left 'Gimme a push start will ya buddy'. Two green-shirted 'deckies' confer about the moving of this VF-1 jet parked in 'fighter country' at the stern of the *Ranger*. The fold away crew ladder and push in doors are all clearly visible, as is the AIM-7 Sparrow medium range missile on the port wing pylon. The yellow tow bar attached to the nose gear leg indicates that this aircraft is one of the alert readiness fighters, prepared for launch should an unidentified aircraft enter the carrier's 'danger zone' (*Tony Holmes*)

Below left The F-14 is a big aircraft, its total all up weight approaching 75,000 lbs when fully loaded with missiles and fuel. Dimensionally the Tomcat is no small fry either; with a 64 foot unswept wingspan and a fuselage length that is not much shorter, it becomes obvious why nose to tail parking is the norm aboard ship. Along with sister-squadron VF-2, the 'Wolfpack' have had more experience on Tomcats than any other frontline unit in the US Navy. Receiving their first F-14s at Miramar in July 1973, the unit went to sea for the first time aboard USS *Enterprise* (CVN-65) in September 1974. Since that first eventful WestPac, which saw the squadron cover the evacuation of Saigon, VF-1 have built up an enviable service record with the aircraft flying with both CVW-14 and CVW-2 aboard three different carriers (*Tony Holmes*)

Below In the early 1980s VF-1 attempted to tone down their Tomcats, as directed by the Chief of Naval Operations (CNO). The glossy grey shades remained the same, but the scarlet fin and fuselage markings were drained of any colour. Luckily for Tomcat enthusiasts, sense prevailed at Miramar and in 1987 permission was given for VF-1 to reinstate the traditional 'Wolfpack' scarlet to their aircraft. Every unit has a CAG aircraft, but none have one quite as bright as this! A late production F-14A built at Calverton in 1985, BuNo 162597 is seen shore-based at NAS Miramar during the summer of 1988 (*John Dibbs*)

Right Having checked that the nose gear tow bar is securely locked into the catapult shuttle, the sailor takes to his heels less than a minute before launch. Now physically part of the ship, this VF-2 'Bounty Hunters' F-14A is carrying not only a Sparrow and a Sidewinder but also a live Phoenix, the latter sitting snuggly in its special mounting beneath the centre fuselage. Having already extended the leading edge slats, the pilot quickly deploys his starboard roll control spoilers to test that they are operable before signalling he is ready to launch (*Tony Holmes*)

Above In marked contrast to traditional VF-2 colours, the squadron was ordered in 1976 to respray several of their aircraft in this fashion, the rather unorthodox scheme being the brainchild of aviation artist Keith Ferris. Seen here at height over the Pacific during its second WestPac with the 'Bounty Hunters', this F-14 (BuNo 158985) clearly shows the aggressive demarcation lines chosen by Ferris to cause altitude deception, especially during dogfights. Extensively evaluated by both the Navy and the Air Force, the scheme was felt to offer no significant benefits over the then current gull grey and white and was therefore never adopted (*US Navy via Bob Archer*)

Above Looking far healthier in standard 'Bounty Hunter' trim, this immaculate Tomcat undergoes preparations for a routine sortie in August 1988. As with the CAG's aircraft, the CO's F-14 is usually maintained in pristine condition also. Belonging to the then BULLET 1, Commander Rip Serhan, this aircraft also wore the name of *Ranger*'s skipper on the canopy, Captain 'Burner' Bob Hickey being a former fighter jock from the Vietnam era (*Tony Holmes*)

Right Carefully placing all the ejector seat safety pins in an appropriately coloured bag, this VF-2 pilot wears the coveted Navy Fighter Weapons School (Top Gun) patch on his left shoulder. The tightness of his G-suit and safety harness can be fully appreciated from this shot. The extension of the famous *Langley* stripes onto the bonedome is a nice touch (*Tony Holmes*)

When the author visited Minamar in the summer of 1988 only two 'Bounty Hunter' Tomcats wore the *Langley* stripe on their fuselage; modex '200' (CAG) and modex '201' (CO). The next aircraft in this nose number sequence can be seen in this photo, and although it wore full colours on the twin fins the stripe is conspicuous by its absence. One of the 'crack' squadrons at Miramar, VF-2 won the annual Fightertown High Noon Gun Derby for the second year running in 1989 (*Tony Holmes*)

As bright as any frontline F-14 unit, VF-2 have managed to retain some colour on their aircraft right through the drab 1980s. The striping below the canopy celebrates the unit's historical links with the original VF-2, and their nickname, '*Langley*', stems from the very first US Navy carrier, USS *Langley*, whose small wooden decks were often home to the 'Bounty Hunters' of the 1930s. Both VF-1 and -2 operate around 24 Tomcats between them, and as is standard naval practice, virtually all of these aircraft will have come from one production batch. Originally issued with very early series (F-14A-80-GR) Tomcats, both squadrons passed their aircraft onto newly transitioned units at Miramar in 1985 and received brand new F-14s in return (*Tony Holmes*)

Left Another squadron not familiar with the term low-viz is VF-21 'Freelancers', one of the last F-4 units in the Navy to transition onto the F-14. Seen here returning from an air combat manoeuvring (ACM) sortie over the Pacific, this Tomcat is devoid of external stores, bar an active seeker tipped AIM-9L dummy Sidewinder round on the port wing shoulder rail (*Frank B Mormillo*)

Above Whilst the rest of the squadron were away at NAS Fallon on a CVW-14 weapons deployment in July 1988, this lone F-14 remained at Miramar as the VF-21 'hanger queen'. Maintenance doors agape beneath the fuselage and inspection panels loosened near the cockpit, FREELANCER 215 is actually engineless, its twin Pratt & Whitney TF30-P-414 turbofans having been removed for a lengthy overhaul. An ex-F3H Demon and F-4 Phantom II squadron, VF-21 received their first F-14s in 1984. An experienced Persian Gulf campaigner with the Tomcat, the 'Freelancers' provided top cover for fleet assets off Iraq for much of 1990 (*John Dibbs*)

Above Sitting pretty on 'Fightertown's' vast ramp, this brand new F-14A had only been on the books of VF-51 'Screaming Eagles' for three months when this classic photo was taken on 16 October 1978. In fact, the 'Eagles' had only been a Tomcat squadron for about the same period of time, having traded in the last of their F-4Ns in early 1978. Already wearing USS *Kitty Hawk* (CV-63) titling on the leading edge of the wing, this F-14 would accompany VF-51 on its first WestPac cruise in May of the following year (*Peter R Foster*)

Left In marked contrast to the previous photo, this stormy shot shows a pale 'Screaming Eagle' living up to its nickname during preflights aboard the brand new USS *Carl Vinson* (CVN-70) in July 1983. Having enjoyed two Seventh Fleet deployments with the *Kitty Hawk*, VF-51, and its controlling body CVW-15, swapped carriers in 1983 to take part in the maiden voyage of the Navy's latest flat top. Possibly enjoying the least colourful period in their long history at this point in time, VF-51 have since managed to add a splash of red and black to the twin fins of their F-14s (*Tom Chee via Bob Archer*)

Above When all around you looks grey, seek out SCREAMING EAGLE 100 and you will find colour in abundance. Although not wearing the full rainbow stripes of former VF-51 CAG aircraft, BuNo 160655 is nevertheless a beauty to behold as it is backed down towards the stern of the *Carl Vinson*. Having just left the picturesque city of Fremantle after a week's R and R, the *Vinson* is steaming up the West Australian coast in the direction of the Philippines, the vessel's next port of call (*Tom Chee via Bob Archer*)

Overleaf Not planning on stopping this time around, a VF-111 'Sundowners' pilot has not extended the tailhook on his F-14. Aboard *Carl Vinson* for the pre-cruise carrier qualification work ups for CVW-15 aircrew, this aircraft logged many missions during the two-week long deployment in November 1985. These 'bump and burns' help the pilot hone his recovery skills to razor sharpness before the actual WestPac commences six weeks later. If you don't make the grade here, you don't make the cruise. The trio of A-6s parked behind the 'frozen' Tomcat belong to VA-52 'Knightriders', CVW-15's heavy attack squadron (*Frank B Mormillo*)

Left Turn the clock back two years from the date of the last photo and the change in VF-111 markings is quite astounding. Wearing perhaps the most famous Tomcat scheme of them all, the shark-mounted 'Sundowners' have been a high visibility asset to the fleet since they received their first F-14s in 1978. Deemed to be far too loud a scheme in the low-viz days of the early 1980s, the setting sun and the gnashers have been scaled down and drained of colour since this shot was taken in July 1983. However, you can't keep a good scheme down for long, VF-111 having recently resprayed their CAG aircraft in full unit colours (*Tom Chee via Bob Archer*)

Left Touching up paint schemes after routine maintenance often adds to the overall effectiveness of an aircraft's camouflage. On an F-14 sprayed up in the tactical greys it just makes the aircraft look scruffy and worn out! The regular mount of an 'all-nugget' (first cruise) crew, this 'Greydowner' Tomcat is enjoying a spot of R and R in Singapore harbour in January 1987 (*Robbie Shaw*)

Below Colourful days on the ramp at NAS Miramar in October 1980. But wait, a low-viz shark mouth has crept into the frame to provide us with a taste of what the future had in store for VF-111. Plenty of scarlet is present on both F-14s, but the traditional sun burst is already missing from '203'. Combat veterans with both the F-8 Crusader and the F-4 Phantom II in the skies over Vietnam, the 'Sundowners' had originally formed in January 1959 on the F11F Tiger. Jumping ahead from that date, 1991 sees VF-111 transitioning onto the ultimate Tomcat, the F-14D, an upgrade that will make them the first west coast fighter squadron equipped with this aircraft (*Frank B Mormillo*)

Left Returning to the ship in a characteristic 'tight two' formation, this pair of VF-114 'Aardvark' F-14s will soon pitch apart and 'go dirty' before recovering aboard USS *Enterprise* (CVN-65). The only squadron in the Navy to paint a false, Ferris-style, cockpit beneath the forward fuselage on the F-14, the 'Aardvarks' obviously felt it gave them an advantage when it came to achieving spatial deception against the enemy during ACM. A quick glance at this shot proves its worth as for a second or two the altitude of these aircraft is open to question because of the dark mass forward of the intakes (*Frank B Mormillo*)

Above Former glory days now but a faded memory, this patchy F-14 once belonged to VF-111 and would have undoubtedly worn the famous nose and fin markings of the squadron at some point in its career. Now, only a partly oversprayed fin flash survives, the remainder of the aircraft having been resprayed. One of several airframes left behind at Miramar by the squadron after they had embarked on board the *Carl Vinson* in the spring of 1988, this particular F-14A was now the property of VF-114 'Aardvarks', hence the respray job (*John Dibbs*)

No doubt about the attitude of this
Tomcat, AARDVARK 114 roaring into the
skies afterburners ignited. From this angle
the sheer size of the main undercarriage
legs can be truly appreciated. Made to
withstand incredible stresses upon landing,
the Bendix designed and built struts were
specially developed for the 'big cat'. The
actual wheels and tyre are from another
source, that great American institution, BF
Goodrich, being the sole contractor for
the Tomcat programme. Like all Tomcat
units of the early 1980s, VF-114 wore a
highly stylized scheme on their aircraft,
the international orange aardvark having
been their trademark since the mid 1950s
(*Frank B Mormillo*)

In contrast, the only splash of colour on this F-14A is the personalized cover fitted over the AXX-1 Northrop Television Camera Set (TCS), mounted beneath the aircraft's radome. Photographed soon after the squadron had been awarded the coveted Admiral Joe Clifton award for being best fighter squadron in the US Navy in 1987, this aircraft wears titling to that effect on the wing shoulder, displacing the standard USS *Enterprise* titling. The Tomcat also wears the Battle Efficiency 'E' and Safety 'S' on its nose, both awards having been presented to the squadron by the Chief of Naval Operations for sustained combat readiness, without injury, over a set period of time (*John Dibbs*)

A luxury at Miramar, permanent hangar space is only allotted to squadrons when they are not at sea. Having just returned from a highly successful WestPac in 1988, VF-114 moved into a hangar vacated by VF-111, the former tennants departing with CVW-15 on their own Pacific Ocean cruise (*John Dibbs*)

Below Belonging to VF-124 'Gunfighters', this weary F-14 has taught its fair share of rookie pilots and RIOs over the years. Charged with the responsibility of turning T-2 Buckeye 'tyros' into Tomcat masters in a six-to eight-month period, VF-124 has the largest complement of F-14s at Miramar. Performing a fast pass over the base before entering the circuit and landing, this Tomcat is configured in typical 'Gunfighters' style – totally storeless. This gives us the chance to examine the fuselage troughs for the AIM-54 Phoenix missile, four of these $5 million weapons fitting beneath the belly of the F-14 (*Tim Laming*)

Left Like sister-squadron VF-101 'Grim Reapers' on the east coast of the USA, VF-124 provide a nominated airshow crew and aircraft for the summer season on the west coast. Performing at hundreds of venues between April and October, this 'NJ' coded 'Gunfighter' is being put through its paces at the Reno Air Races in 1987. The four strakes in the mid section of the aircraft serve the dual purpose of both stiffening the overall wing glove area and providing effective channels for the air to flow more efficiently over the upper fuselage of the Tomcat (*Steve Mansfield*)

Above Gear firmly locked down, a trainee pilot commences his approach to Miramar. All landings made by naval aviators ashore are tackled just as if they were recovering aboard a carrier at sea. This means no flaring out before touch down, the pilot aiming for an imaginary three-wire painted across the black top. Without the almost mandatory belly tanks fitted beneath each intake, this VF-124 F-14 looks rather emaciated (*Tim Laming*)

Right 'Boo!' Compressed by the photographer's telephoto lens, a recently arrived 'Gunfighters' F-14 looms over a tow tractor at Marine Corps Air Station El Toro in May 1989. Performing airshow duties yet again, this F-14 wears a typically high training squadron modex on its nose. Besides flying the standard model Tomcat, VF-124 also operates the uprated A+(Plus) version, and will soon be adding examples of the F-14D to its ranks as well (*Frank B Mormillo*)

Left A relative newcomer to the Tomcat when compared to the 'Gunfighters' of VF-124, the 'Black Knights' of VF-154 completed their transition onto the Grumman fighter in 1984. Firmly attached to a yellow 'mule', this aircraft is being respotted further down the ramp at Miramar, its refuelling probe extended alongside the canopy. Attached to CVW-14 and the USS *Constellation* (CV-64) since receiving the Tomcat, the squadron, and its controlling airwing, recently transferred to USS *Independence* (CV-62), the 'Connie' going into drydock for an extensive refit (*Frank B Mormillo*)

Above A nondescript 'Gunfighters' F-14A bakes in the summer sun at Miramar, canopy agape to keep the ambient temperature within the cockpit a little below boiling point. Flown heavily all year round, it's not uncommon to see six or eight VF-124 Tomcats droning around the station in an endless circuit. taking it in turns to 'bump and burn' during carrier landing practice. The very first Navy squadron to receive the Tomcat, VF-124 began work ups with the aircraft in October 1972. In earlier times, the unit had trained pilots to fly the classical F-8 Crusader (*John Dibbs*)

Right Showing the current scheme off to perfection, this drab F-14A slowly closes on Miramar's main strip. Operating some of the oldest F-14s in the fleet, most VF-213 aircraft were built about 15 years ago. Since the North Island shot was taken in 1988, the black lion emblem on the tail has been altered somewhat, the ferocious beast now sporting a much fuller mane (*Tim Laming*)

Below Considering its colour, this motif could only belong to one rather appropriately named Tomcat squadron, VF-213 'Black Lions'. An experienced Tomcat operator since 1976, the 'Lions' once adorned their aircraft with lashings of blue and gold paint, but alas no more. A former F-4 squadron, VF-213 modified their emblem slightly by doubling the number of tails on the lion to better reflect the 'tail feathers' of their new mount. Seen at the NAS North Island Naval Air Rework Facility (NARF) in 1988, this Tomcat had been customized by a nameless individual who had a penchanct for Playboy bunny ears. Could he have been a member of a certain Marine Corps Prowler unit that will remain nameless? (*John Dibbs*)

Atlantic, the Med and Oceana

The state of Virginia has been linked with the US Navy since the earliest days of the Union, the dark Atlantic waters off its craggy coastline having witnessed the first skirmishes between warships flying the stars and stripes, and vessels of the mighty Royal Navy.

Having matured into a fighting force unrivalled by any other fleet, the modern US Navy still has a formidable presence in Virginia, its burgeoning base at Norfolk being the homeport of more warships than any other facility of its type in the world. The largest of the vessels based at Norfolk are the supercarriers assigned to the Sixth Fleet, their regular six-month deployments taking them across the Atlantic and into the Mediterranean and Arabian seas on 'policing' patrols.

An integral part of the air wing embarked on these vessels is also based in the beautiful state of Virginia. The large master jet base at NAS Oceana is home to 13 Tomcat squadrons who in total operate no less than 200 aircraft. Responsible for the defence of both the air wing and the fleet, the squadrons at Oceana are amongst the longest serving fighter units in the world today. Squadrons like VF-11 'Red Rippers' and VF-31 'Tomcatters' have been flying Grumman fighters since the early 1930s, their parent air wings having been a part of naval aviation for a similar period of time.

Although Miramar and 'Top Gun' has stolen the limelight from Oceana and its Tomcat squadrons over the years, the fact remains that Norfolk-based F-14 units are still the only members of the fighter clan to have notched up a score with the Grumman fighter. As the pilots and RIOs are so fond of saying down Norfolk way, 'At Miramar they make films. At Oceana we make history!'

F-14 Tomcat Squadrons at NAS Oceana

VF-11	'Red Rippers'	VF-41	'Black Aces'	VF-103	'Sluggers'
VF-14	'Tophatters'	VF-74	'Be-devilers'	VF-142	'Ghostriders'
VF-31	'Tomcatters'	VF-84	'Jolly Rogers'	VF-143	'Pukin' Dogs'
VF-32	'Swordsmen'	VF-101	'Grim Reapers'		
VF-33	'Tarsiers'	VF-102	'Diamondbacks'		

Closing rapidly on the hard steel of USS *Forrestal's* (CV-59) deck, this VF-11 'Red Rippers' F-14 is being closely scrutinized by the clutch of experienced landing signals officers (LSO) that frequent the stern of a carrier during air wing recoveries. One of these high time lieutenants will be a 'Red Ripper', his job being to help guide the Tomcat jock back aboard ship. Every landing made during a cruise is given a grade depending on its accuracy; an OK recovery translates to an excellent landing; fair is a safe but not brilliant trap; no grade is hazardous to one's career as a naval aviator; and cut basicallly mean you are lucky to be back aboard with your boots dry! In Navy speak this appears to be an OK approach (*Angelo Romano*)

Left Buried deeply within the bulkheads of the carrier are the squadron ready rooms, sacred territory to pilots, RIOs and associated air wing colleagues. Each embarked unit aboard ship has its own ready room, the small area usually bedecked in squadron colours, its walls adorned with souvenirs 'won' during past cruises. This tiny enclave hidden in the bowels of the *Forrestal* is 'Red Ripper' country. Here, VF-11 pilots are getting the gouge on useful dogfighting techniques should a MiG-29 'Fulcrum' happen to stray across their bows whilst cruising above the Med (*Angelo Romano*)

Above Whilst its crew is enjoying a spot of R and R in Marseille, this F-14A has just received an early morning rub down on the stern of *Forrestal*. A relative newcomer to the Tomcat, VF-11 first deployed to the Med aboard USS *John F Kennedy* (CV-67) in 1982 (*Yves Debay*)

F-14 Tomcat

Right Scanning the clear blue skies in search of 'enemy' fighters, a pair of 'Red Rippers' cruise along at height in their F-14. Hiding in the haze are Tunisian F-5E Tiger I Is, this small African nation providing the adversaries for today's ACM sortie. Small, nimble and quick, the F-5 can be a handful for the large Tomcat if flown skilfully by its pilot. Although not quite as good as the fighter weapons school jocks back at Miramar, the Tunisians were nevertheless described as worthy opponents during the *Forrestal's* 1990 Med cruise, the outcome of this particular sortie remaining classified! (*Lieutenant B Herdlick via Angelo Romano*)

Above In between cruises, this toned down Tomcat is brought back 'aboard' NAS Oceana after a gunnery exercise off the Virginian coastline. Having loosened off a few rounds from its internal General Electric M61A1 20 mm cannon, the Tomcat's gun port beneath the modex is particularly dirty. Capable of firing up to 6000 rounds per minute, the M61A1 is fed by a 675-round magazine drum fitted immediately below the RIO's feet. An important addition to the Tomcat's arsenal, the cannon was specifically requested by the Navy when it issued its requirement for a Phantom I I replacement in the late 1960s. Like most Tomcat squadrons of today, VF-11 flew both the Crusader and the F-4 Phantom I I before receiving its first Grumman 'swingers' in the summer of 1980 (*Peter R Foster*)

Left Although not obvious from this angle, the Tomcat in the middle of this Grumman 'sandwich' belongs to VF-32 'Swordsmen', whilst its companions on either side are VF-14 'Tophatters' F-14s. Tightly packed near the island on board USS *John F Kennedy* (CV-67), all three aircraft have their wings pinned back in the seven degree 'oversweep' position, a novel feature built into the F-14 by the manufacturers to allow the Navy to embark up to 24 of these heavy weight fighters on a super carrier. The key to the Tomcat's incredible agility at both high and low speeds is clearly visible in this shot; the huge flat area of wing and fuselage which endear the aircraft with buckets of lift. Unfortunately, this same wide space of Tomcat is also more prone to weathering than any other area! (*Angelo Romano*)

Above Although now darker than it has ever been in the past, the famous top hat motif has adorned naval aircraft longer than any other symbol in the modern fleet. Originally an attack squadron, VF-14 can trace its lineage back to September 1919. However, the modern 'Tophatters' were only redesignated a fighter squadron in December 1949, the squadron initially receiving the classic F4U-5 Corsair at Jacksonville, Florida. Flying such varied types as the F3D-2 Skyknight and the F3H-2 Demon during the 1950s, VF-14 finally got their hands on a fighter worthy of their talents in 1963 when the first F-4B Phantom IIs arrived at their Cecil Field home. After a decade of operations with the F-4B, the squadron became the first east coast fighter unit to transition onto the F-14A at Miramar. A unit with a long and colourful history, VF-14 continue to perform their daring deeds in the 1990s aboard the '*JFK*' as part of CVW-3 (*Yves Debay*)

Left Unfortunately not all 'Tomcatters' F-14s survived the advent of low-viz unscathed, this particular aircraft, seen aboard the *Forrestal* in January 1990, having a slate grey rather than glossy black radome. Although a large beast when on the deck, the Tomcat still retains some degree of manoeuvrability through its fully steerable nosewheel. Preparing for a launch off bow cat one, the pilot of this aircraft has lined his wheels up with the catapult track, the rest of the Tomcat swinging into line as he 'drives' the fighter up the deck *(Robbie Shaw)*

Above Almost as old and arguably as famous as VF-14 are the high fliers of VF-31, the second oldest fighter squadron in the US Navy. Having a penchant for black noses, the 'Tomcatters' have managed to continue this tradition on into the 1990s with their fleet of suitably decorated F-14s. Soon to depart on a CAP over *Forrestal's* battlegroup, this CAG F-14 is undergoing its final preflight checks by both the crew and the plane captain. Rather appropriately, this Tomcat appears to have been christened 'Felix' *(Angelo Romano)*

Left The jet blast deflectors (JBDs) are raised, the catapult tow bar is firmly attached to the shuttle, the wings are fully spread and the leading edge slats are drooped to their maximum position. All that remains now is for the cat crewman to scurry away from the nosegear of the Tomcat. The pilot will then commence his afterburner checks before signalling to the deck officer that he is ready to launch. Meanwhile, the green-shirt in the deck trough will have been keeping an eye on the steam pressure for waist cat two, signalling to both the crew and the deck officer when the catapult has built up enough power for launch (*Angelo Romano*)

Above The detailed finish on the squadron CAG bird even stretches to customized drop tanks. The tyre manufacturer's name has also been picked out in white paint on the main undercarriage gear. The complexity of the mid fuselage area on the F-14 is clearly shown in this view, the lack of space between the missile pylon, undercarriage door, undercarriage leg and the belly tank being particularly noticeable (*Angelo Romano*)

Right Amongst the predominantly grey aircraft packed onto *Forrestal's* deck, the blood red tails of VF-31's Tomcats stand out clearly. Although an assortment of A-6s, A-7s and S-3s are jammed onto the stern of the vessel, this area is usually reserved for the fighter squadrons embarked on the ship. A grand old lady of the sea, *Forrestal* was the first supercarrier commissioned into the Navy, and the name-ship of this four-carrier class. Now well over 30 years old, the vessel has undergone extensive refits over the years to allow it to operate modern naval aircraft, the last SLEP (Service Life Extension Programme) ending in early 1986 (*Angelo Romano*)

Below Multi-petal exhaust nozzles fully open, the rasping TF30s lick the JBD with orange flames as the pilot initiates phase five afterburner by pushing the throttles forward. He will open and close the nozzles, testing the engines in all power regimes to check that one powerplant is not surging over the other, before finally turning up the wick and signalling he is ready for launch. The cat officer (white shirt) kneeling behind the F-14 is signalling that all is well with the tail end of the Tomcat, the nozzles opening and closing as they should. The white line several feet behind him marks the border of the safety zone, no man's land being to the left of that thin strip during launches (*Angelo Romano*)

Right Having snagged a two-wire, a colourful F-14 from VF-32 'Swordsmen' comes back aboard the *John F Kennedy* in November 1975. Participating in the first Atlantic cruise for an Oceana-based Tomcat squadron, VF-32, along with sister-squadron VF-14, had a highly satisfactory deployment aboard the '*JFK*', so much so that they were awarded the Admiral Joseph Clifton trophy for being the top fighter squadron in the Navy for 1975. The extremely wavy demarcation line between the undersurface white and the gull grey of the upper fuselage and wings was as much a distinguishing feature on VF-32 Tomcats as the bright yellow twin fins during the squadron's early years with the Grumman fighter (*Angelo Romano*)

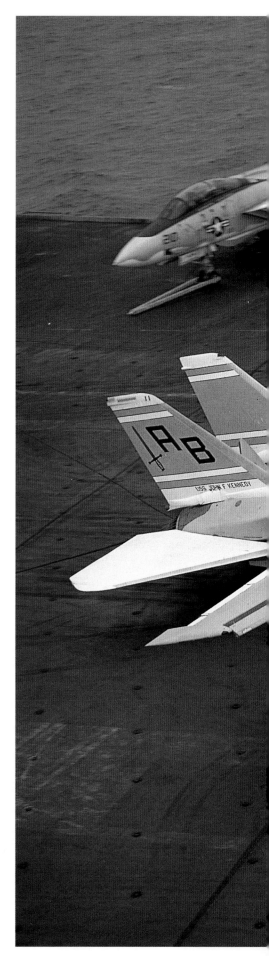

Above Now back aboard their traditional floating home, VF-32 rejoined the '*JFK*' and CVW-3 in 1985, this partnership continuing on into the 1990s. Exhibiting a distinct lack of colour when photographed in November 1988, the markings on this F-14A are a far cry from the glory days of the squadron in the mid seventies. Two months after this photo was taken, F-14s from VF-32 hit world headlines when a pair of 'Swordsmen' Tomcats downed a pair of Libyan Air Force MiG-23MS *Flogger Es* over the Med after an aggressive confrontation between the fighters that lasted approximately nine minutes. Besides the 'Black Aces' of VF-41, the 'Swordsmen' are the only other F-14 unit to have blooded the Grumman fighter in combat (*Angelo Romano*)

Left Seven years later and the glowing fins have been toned down somewhat, replaced by a larger sword and horizontal bars. Part of CVW-6, VF-32 spent much of the early eighties aboard USS *Independence* (CV-62), the squadron being heavily involved during this 1983 cruise supporting the US Navy task force off the Lebanese coast. In fact, a TARPS (Tactical Air Reconnaissance Pod System) equipped F-14A from VF-32 flew a bomb damage assessment sortie over targets hit by A-6s and A-7s during the inconclusive Alpha strike flown in December 1983, the recce-Tomcat coming under fire from Syrian positions during the mission (*Angelo Romano*)

Above From the last Atlantic fleet squadron to bag a MiG in combat to the first. Although equipped with a totally different aeroplane, VF-33 'Tarsiers' nevertheless became the first east coast MiG killers on 10 July 1968 when an F-4J Phantom I I crewed by Lieutenant Roy Cash Jr and Lieutenant Joseph Kain Jr downed a MiG-21 with an AIM-9 Sidewinder. Now enjoying more peaceful cruises, the 'Tarsiers', or 'Starfighters' as they are sometimes called, having been Tomcat operators since 1981. Equipped with some of the oldest F-14s in current frontline service, the squadron has nevertheless formed an integral part of CVW-1's offensive capabilities over the past decade. Beginning to look its age, this blotchy 'Starfighter' still wears some colour on its twin fins nevertheless. Parked amongst suitably decorated VF-102 'Diamondback' F-14s aboard USS *America* (CV-66), this veteran 'Starfighter' was enjoying a spot of R and R whilst the carrier was anchored off Spithead, near Portsmouth, in September 1985 (*Bob Archer*)

F-14 Tomcat

Right Aside from the 'Tomcatters' of VF-31, only one other unit has ever 'blacked out' the radomes on their F-14s, albeit for a very brief period of time. The appropriately named 'Black Aces' of VF-41 wore this attractive scheme on their Tomcats for about four years, the squadron applying unit colours to the F-14s as they arrived at Oceana from the Grumman factory at Calverton in 1976. Whilst the pilot expresses his feelings of 'friendship' towards the photographer, the RIO snatches a glance at the craggy Italian landscape below. Wearing full squadron colours, this F-14 was embarked on board USS *Nimitz* (CVN-68) during VF-41's maiden Atlantic cruise with the Tomcat in 1977/78 (*Angelo Romano*)

Below Back in more familiar surroundings, this VF-33 Tomcat is returning to NAS Oceana after an ACM sortie with a VF-43 'Challengers' F-16N out over the Atlantic. The only item of colour on this drab aircraft is the dayglo orange telemetry pod fitted beneath the wing pylon. The 'Starfighters' participated in the 'Around the Horn' cruise of USS *Constellation* (CV-64) in early 1990, VF-33 being the only fighter squadron temporarily attached to a composite CVW-9 for *Connie*'s SLEP trip to Norfolk naval dockyard (*Peter R Foster*)

Below Also photographed during the maiden voyage, this F-14A wears the '100' modex that denotes it as being the CAG's personal aircraft. In front of the Tomcat is a large AIM-54 Phoenix missile, and beneath its port wing are two trolleys loaded with AIM-7 Sparrows and AIM-9 Sidewinders (*Angelo Romano*)

Left And this is what a fully loaded wing pylon looks like after the squadron red shirts (ordnance men) have finished with it. Alternatively, a larger pylon can be slotted into this spot and a Phoenix round bolted on. Covered with a seeker head protector, this Sidewinder is an early D-model weapon, Ford Aerospace having built over 950 of these semi active radar homing (SARH) rounds specially for the Navy. Fitting snugly into the purpose built pylon beneath the Sidewinder is a Raytheon AIM-7F Sparrow, a somewhat temperamental medium range missile currently being superceded by the far more potent AIM-120A AMRAAM (*Angelo Romano*)

Left The sun is low and the shadows are long as an armed up Tomcat is towed 'sternward' in the early morning light. Once 'spotted' on the stern, the crew will be informed that FAST EAGLE 105 is ready to go, and they will walk to the aircraft as soon as they are suited-up (*Angelo Romano*)

Above It is amazing how quickly things can change in US naval aviation circles when it comes to paint schemes. This is how things looked when next the *Nimitz* sailed into the Med in late 1979, the 'Black Aces' having embraced the blanket order to tone down the Tomcat quicker than any other squadron in the Navy. Besides looking downright boring when compared to its former glory days of 1978, this drab Tomcat is also suffering from wing box pivot problems, as well as having had its port TF30 dropped out the bottom of the engine bay for an extensive overhaul. Not normally used as an 'open air' garage, the flightdeck on the *Nimitz* is being utilized by VF-41 maintainers whilst the carrier is in Naples harbour during an R and R stop over (*Angelo Romano*)

F-14 Tomcat

BARCAP completed, the squadron CO's F-14 is brought back aboard the 'steel Teddy', its glossy scheme contrasting markedly with other VF-41 aircraft. Now allowed to wear muted squadron colours on two aircraft, most fighter units have resprayed both the CAG's and the CO's Tomcats in glossy finish. In fact, Grumman were specifically requested by the Navy to deliver the final batch of A-model F-14s in this glossy light grey scheme so that these aircraft could be issued to the various squadrons ready for customizing at unit level. This meant that squadrons didn't have to strip off freshly applied drab greys and then respray a perfectly good aircraft in gloss colours. Thus, FAST EAGLE 101 was one of the younger Tomcats embarked on 'TR' during its maiden cruise in early 1989 (*Jean-Pierre Montbazet*)

Right Having been assigned to CVW-8 and the *Nimitz* since transitioning onto the Tomcat in 1976, VF-41, and its associated air wing, got to move ships in 1988 when they were transferred to the brand new nuclear carrier USS *Theodore Roosevelt* (CVN-72), the squadron's former 'mobile home' being transferred to the Pacific fleet. Firmly attached to waist cat one, this drab VF-41 Tomcat is about to be launched on yet another BARCAP (Barrier Combat Air Patrol) in defence of '*TR's*' battle group during *exercise Phinia '89*, a large event involving the French Navy (*Jean-Pierre Montbazet*)

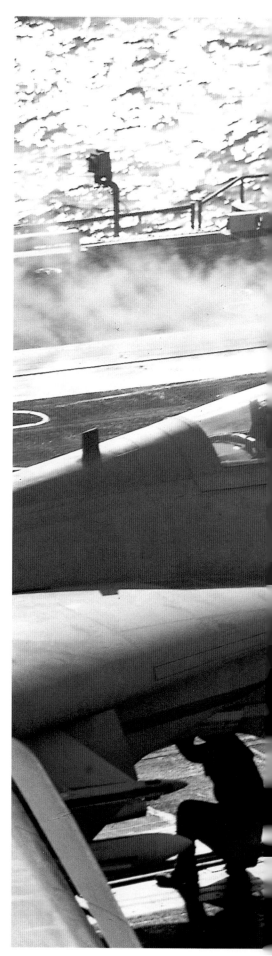

Above Sharing the fighter duties with VF-41 during *Nimitz's* European tour in 1977/78 was VF-84 'Jolly Rogers', the former F-4N operators having transitioned onto the Tomcat at Oceana alongside the 'Black Aces'. Partners since 1959, VF-84 and -41 have shared many a Med cruise aboard the *Independence*, the *Franklin D Roosevelt*, the *Nimitz* and finally the *Theodore Roosevelt*. Going back 13 years to VF-84's first Med cruise with the Tomcat, we see the squadron's CAG bird being towed into position for a launch from waist cat one. Behind the glossy F-14, two equally colourful S-3A Vikings from VS-24 'Scouts' await their turn in the launch cycle. Like the fighter boys, the sub hunters of VS-24 were also experiencing their first cruise with CVW-8 and *Nimitz* (*Angelo Romano*)

Left Unlike VF-41, the 'Jolly Rogers' have always maintained some colour on their F-14s. Taxiing down the deck before launch, this grey beauty has no TCS pod fitted beneath its radome, although the mandatory Sanders ALQ-100 noise deception jammer and positional light are present. Now replaced by the vastly upgraded AN/ALQ-126A or B sensor, the small blister still has the same external dimensions. The catapult launch ball mounted at the end of the nose gear strop is also visible in this view (*Angelo Romano*)

Above 'Wallop!' The CO of VF-84 brings his pristine mount back aboard ship. The leading edge slats, combined with the variable sweep wings, give the F-14 an over the ramp speed of about 130 knots, a far more civilized figure than the 140+ for the F-4 and the near suicidal 150 for the F-8 Crusader. The spool up response of the twin TF30s is also far better than that ever achieved with the powerplants of either the F-4 or F-8; a comforting thought for naval aviators on both coasts (*Angelo Romano*)

Left Clean and mean, a storeless Tomcat comes in close for a better look at the photographer's camera-ship. Rather surprisingly, this particular F-14 has no crew names emblazoned on the canopy rail. Typically for this period in Tomcat operations, no body hugging external tanks are fitted to the aircraft, this optional accessory only becoming fashionable with fleet squadrons in the early eighties (*Angelo Romano*)

Above With a pair of finless 270 gallon tanks firmly bolted to its underbelly, the CAG's F-14 prepares to be struck down below decks aboard the 'TR'. A late build Tomcat delivered from Calverton in the glossy grey scheme previously mentioned, the aircraft has a definite mid-seventies feel about it due to the unsprayed glass-fibre radome. Earlier on in the Med cruise, VF-84 was awarded the coveted CNO Battle 'E', all squadron aircraft being suitably adorned with the highly prized letter soon after the trip commenced. Because of the large size of the aircraft, about a quarter of the Tomcat usually hangs out over the edge of the lift when the time comes to take it below deck for maintenance (*Jean-Pierre Montbazet*)

Previous pages Holding station alongside a pale VF-41 F-14, the crew of JOLLY ROGER 201 occupy themselves with last minute checks before being marshalled up to one of the waist cats. The 'deckie' is giving the aircraft a quick visual once over to make sure that no fluid is leaking from the engines and that all maintenance panels are firmly fastened. The small oval shaped hole near the base of the fin is a cooling air louvre for the afterburner ducting, whilst the rectangular troughs on the wing shoulders are intake duct spill doors (*Jean-Pierre Montbazet*)

Above Whilst the pilot leans forward to check that his shoulder harnesses are suitably tight, the RIO glances down at the cat crew, both of whom are scanning the underside of the CAG Tomcat. As clean as they come, this F-14 has the latest model of Phoenix missile strapped to its belly, the uprated AIM-54C. Developed by Hughes in 1977 to meet Navy needs for the 1990s, the C-model missile has new all-digital electronics which make the Phoenix a more flexible and reliable system. Solid state technology has meant that the klystron

tube DSQ-26 planar active radar has been replaced with a new system. Nortronics have upgraded the inertial reference unit within the missile and the weapon's electronic counter-countermeasures (ECCM) capabilities have also been improved. Finally, development work undertaken by the Navy Weapons Center has resulted in a new proximity fuse being fitted to the missile. Wearing a yellow band around its midriff, this particular Phoenix round is live (*Jean-Pierre Montbazet*)

Perhaps more representative of VF-84 drab in the 1990s, this Tomcat is parked near the stern of 'TR'. Not quite as photogenic as '200' or '201', this aircraft is perhaps even more interesting for the serious aviation enthusiast because of the strong demarcation line between the two greys used in the overall low-viz scheme. A feature so far only seen on 'Jolly Rogers' Tomcats, the merging of the two greys is usually far more subtle. The trolley in front of the aircraft is loaded up with live, but finless, AIM-7M medium range missiles. (Jean-Pierre Montbazet)

Right The crew look on as their armed Tomcat is respotted after completing yet another mission during exercise *Phinia '89*. Flying air combat sorties against 'enemy' F-8 Crusaders and Super Etendards of the French Aeronavale, VF-84 used the exercise to gain valuable combat knowledge about types they wouldn't normally encounter (*Jean-Pierre Montbazet*)

Above Still flying the 'Jolly Roger', albeit in low-viz colours, VF-84 owe their distinctive tail insignia and nickname to former ramp mates, VF-61, this late lamented squadron unofficially beqeathing them over to VF-84 when they disbanded in 1959 (*Jean-Pierre Montbazet*)

A drab Tomcat taxies over the flush JBD and onto the catapult track seconds after another CVW-8 aircraft has launched from the cat alongside. In more colourful times VF-84 gained notoriety by 'splashing' two Japanese Zeroes in the Hollywood hit 'The Final Countdown'. Getting back to reality, the 'Jolly Rogers' made history with their own film, albeit of the 'still' type, in 1981 when they took the TARPS pod to sea for the first time, the successful completion of this cruise clearing the system for sull-scale squadron use by both Oceana- and Miramar-based units
(*Jean-Pierre Montbazet*)

Attached to the oldest air wing in the US Navy, VF-102 'Diamondbacks' have been a part of CVW-1 since they first received the Tomcat at Oceana in 1982. The final F-4J 'Phlyers' in the Navy, the 'Diamondbacks' never really had a chance to fully exploit the F-14 when it came to squadron colours, drab grey being the uniform of the day by the time the first 'Diamondback' Tomcats arrived at Oceana. Nevertheless, the squadron has adopted a busy scheme for their aircraft, a brief flirtation with blood red diamonds having now been superceded by traditional eightie's style grey 'jewels' on the forward fuselage and wing glove leading edges. The traditional two-letter fin code in the diamond was finally replaced in 1988 by a detailed rendition of the squadron's unit badge itself, although the non-standard application of the titling 'USA' at the base of each rudder mysteriously appeared on VF-102's aircraft during USS *America's* (CV-66) Med cruise in 1989 (*Robert F Dorr*)

Left above & below 'Puke' and 'Ratbreath' are marshalled up towards the waist cat on *America* as the carrier steams across the Atlantic towards the Med. Although not exhibiting much taste when it comes to call-signs, this VF-102 pairing are arguably the best team in the squadron when it comes to 'hassling' in the Tomcat. Both having attained the rank of commander, the total accumulated flying hours of this pair would be well over 5000. Befitting an aircraft carrying a '101' modex, this F-14A is painted in glossy colours, although the 'Diamondbacks' idea of a high-viz scheme is not going to set the world alight (*Both photos by Robert F Dorr*)

Above A long way from the Atlantic, DIAMONDBACK 112 pulls alongside a KA-6D tanker from VA-34 'Blue Blasters' over the scorched earth near NAS Fallon, Nevada, during CVW-1 work-ups in December 1983. Totally devoid of any external stores, this F-14A, BuNo 161285, was one of 30 Tomcats ordered in Fiscal Year (FY) 1980. The Navy has always tried to keep batches of aircraft together at squadron level, this policy resulting in roughly half of the FY 80 F-14s being sent straight from Calverton to NAS Oceana in late 1981, the Tomcats being issued to VF-102 as they reformed on the new Grumman fighter after retiring their weary F-4Js (*Dave Parsons via Angelo Romano*)

F-14 Tomcat

Sister-ship to the previous Tomcat, this
'Diamondback' F-14 carries slightly more
ordnance than its squadron mate, a live
AIM-7 and AIM-54 firmly fixed to the
shoulder pylon and underbelly respectively.
Painted up in a scheme typical of VF-102 in
their first 18 months as Tomcat operators,
this aircraft even has the traditional red
diamonds emblazoned upon its external
tanks (*via Angelo Romano*)

Left Come January 1986, BuNo 161286 was still wearing unlucky '113' on its nose, but the traditional red diamonds had long since faded to grey. Carrying a single telemetry pod on the port wing shoulder and what appears to be a semi-gloss grey external tank, the F-14 cruises between layers of cloud high above the Med. The pilot is maintaining his spatial awareness by scanning out of the canopy whilst the RIO appears to be preoccupied with his starboard cockpit console, perhaps the ECM or IFF (identification friend or foe) transponders having alerted him to a potential threat
(*Lt Cdr Dave Parsons via Angelo Romano*)

Above Before Tomcat tyros are let anywhere near a carrier deck or a fleet squadron they join the ranks of VF-101 'Grim Reapers', the Atlantic fleet replacement air group (RAG) unit. Charged with the responsibility of shaping inexperienced naval aviators into razor sharp Tomcat crews in under eight months, the instructors at VF-101 are amongst the best F-14 operators around. The experience of the instructor comes into play throughout the pupil's course, especially when it comes to mastering the basics like carrier landings or, as in this case, air-to-air refuelling. Taking it in turns to 'plug in' then disengage high over the Norfolk coastline, this drab pair of F-14s are enjoying the hospitality of an equally anonymous KA-6D from VA-35 'Black Panthers'. The location of the retractable probe alongside the forward cockpit gives the pilot an unequalled view when it comes to refuelling (*Stuart Black*)

Left A pretender to the throne? A brown-shirted plane captain goes about checking the vertical display indicator (VDI) controls on the starboard console of the CAG-ship from VF-142 'Ghostriders'. He is sitting on a Martin-Baker GRU7A rocket assisted zero/zero ejection seat, this particular mark of British 'throne' having been fitted to the Tomcat early on in the programme. The lustreless finish of the low-viz scheme on current fleet Tomcats is well illustrated in this close-up shot (*Steve Mansfield*)

Above Wearing their cranials and goggles, a group of red-shirted squadron armourers look on as the CO's F-14A+(Plus) gets its tanks topped up before taxying to the catapult. Interestingly, the refuelling probe on this aircraft, and the one behind it, is deployed, indicating that the crew are performing a quick preflight check on this vital piece of apparatus before launch. As with many Tomcat units on both sides of America, VF-142 is currently led by a RIO, Commander 'Ham' Tallent being a high time 'Ghostrider' from way back (*Steve Mansfield*)

F-14 Tomcat

Right Checks completed, tanks full and tie down chains safely stored, the pilot blips the throttle on GHOSTRIDER 201 and taxies the aircraft forward towards the bow cats. The F-14 crew is never left to wander the cramped deck aimlessly, their progress down the pitching steel being carefully monitored by strategically placed air wing handlers who pass the Tomcat from one yellow-shirt to the next until the aircraft is firmly attached to the catapult shuttle. The crew of '201' are being directed towards bow cat one, aboard USS *Dwight D Eisenhower* (CVN-69), as the carrier sails in the Med during exercise *Dragon Hammer '90* (*Steve Mansfield*)

Above Two years before, during *Dragon Hammer '88*, VF-142 had two F-14s in full-colour unit markings, modex '200' and '201' being the obvious candidates for this treatment. Here, '201' is carefully attached to the catapult launch shuttle on the bow of '*Ike*'. With the arrival of updated A+(Plus) Tomcats at Oceana in late 1989, VF-142 relinquished its fleet of standard F-14As, including the two 'glossies', for 14 drab grey airframes (*Yves Debay*)

And they don't come much drabber than this 'Ghostrider', minutes away from launch. The 1990 Med cruise for VF-142 and CVW-7 marked the debut of the A+(Plus) in Mediterranean waters, the 'Ghostriders' reporting favourably on the behaviour of their new mounts both on the deck and in the air (*Steve Mansfield*)

Less spectacular than the old F-14A when it comes to launches, the A+(Plus) can safely rotate from a carrier deck in military power, thus increasing the range of the Tomcat appreciably. The afterburner cans on the aircraft have been completely redesigned for the installation of the twin General Electric F110-GE-400 turbofans, the nozzles now being appreciably larger than those fitted for the TF30s. Another mod introduced with the A+(Plus) is the enlarged ECM transmitter aerial that has appeared alongside the fuel dump vent on the beaver tail between the fins. Operating on different wavebands from those covered by the fin tip emitters, the excresence is part of the Sanders AN/ALQ-126 system, these bulges also being retrofitted to earlier F-14As (*Steve Mansfield*)

F-14 Tomcat

Right A sight to warm the hearts (literally) of Tomcat fans everywhere, a VF-142 F-14A departs on another sortie during *Dragon Hammer '88*. The visual difference between the A and the A+(Plus) in launch mode is perfectly illustrated by this shot; the rasping orange flames of the TF30 in full phase five afterburner clearly denoting the older powerplant. Compared to the 27,000 lbs of static thrust produced by each F110, the TF30 can only offer 20,900 lbs in its most developed form (*Yves Debay*)

Above This is what makes carrier aviation the unique occupation that it is; breakneck launches from zero to 160 knots in a flash of grey metal and wispy steam. Scorching down the deck, the 65,000 lb Tomcat prepares to be flung off the '*Ike*' and into the clear blue Sardinian sky. Just visible in the rear cockpit is the ungloved hand of the RIO, his fingers firmly gripping the instrument coaming in front of him. In comparison to the last shot, the afterburner nozzles have been retracted inwards for the launch cycle (*Steve Mansfield*)

F-14 Tomcat

The shuttle firmly stopped against the rubber butts at the end of the cat rail, the carrier steams on at 30 knots whilst the Tomcat claws its way skywards at a speed approaching six times that figure. The lack of flame emanating from the back end of a Tomcat makes for less spectacular launches, although the crews who are strapped into these aircraft don't mind the lack of fireworks one little bit! (*Steve Mansfield*)

Left Well and truly in the groove, a VF-142 pilot glides in over the ramp of the '*Ike*' at dusk, the familiar sooty trial of the twin TF30s marking his path behind him. In the foreground, the LSO from the squadron carefully talks him down towards the carrier, the vital role played by this seasoned naval aviator increasing in importance as the sun dips away beneath the horizon. The Tomcat would be approaching the '*Ike*' at about 130 knots at this point, the pilot using a fine blend of throttle and stick to maintain the correct glidepath approach (*Yves Debay*)

Above Awaiting its crew on a crowded deck, a colourless F-14A+(Plus) sits with its huge one-piece canopy cranked back to reduce heat build up in the cockpit. Silhouetted against the perspex are the vital rear view mirrors, the pilot having three affixed to the forward canopy framing whilst the RIO makes do with a single one. Although the crews twist and turn in their seats to try and keep a visual check on 'bogeys' during ACM, the firmness of the the harness and cramped confines of the cockpit itself limit the crew's ability to move, hence the vital role played by the small strip mirrors (*Steve Mansfield*)

Right Surrounded by an assortment of air- and deckcrew, the plane captain of modex '111' vacates the cockpit and prepares to ease himself down towards the deck. The newest airframe embarked aboard 'Ike' during the carrier's Med cruise in 1990, this aircraft (BuNo 163220) belongs to the tastefully named 'Pukin Dogs' of VF-143. Besides the remodelled afterburner nozzles, the F-14A+(Plus) also features new air intakes for the nose mounted M61A1 cannon, the former slatted vents beneath the cockpit having been replaced by smaller, but more effective, troughs over the barrel of the weapon itself. A new intake trough has appeared over the breach of the weapon. The revised gun gas purge system was specifically requested by the Navy when Grumman was contracted to develop an updated version of the F-14. This particular Tomcat was exhibited at the 1990 Battle of Britain Airshow at Boscombe Down (*Steve Mansfield*)

Below CAG and D-CAG taxy down towards the stern of 'Ike' to join the queue awaiting the next cycle of launches during *Dragon Hammer '90*. The air boss usually staggers deck ops to allow the ship's captain to make full use of the embarked air wing, one group of aircraft returning to the ship just after a replacement group has launched. On a good day the launch and recovery of two separate batches of 20 aircraft can usually be accomplished in under 15 minutes (*Steve Mansfield*)

Left 'I thought he said go that way!' Two blotchy F-14As pass each other on the slippery deck as the aircraft from CVW-7 jostle for position, awaiting their turn to launch. The Tomcat closest to the camera appears to be suffering from a jammed catapult strop, several 'deckies' milling around the forward gear leg offering their opinion on how to free the offending article. Minor problems like this one cause major headaches for the air boss as each aircraft is allotted a certain launch time in a sequence which fits in with mission requirements. A certain amount of slack is built into the launch cycle by the 'boss' to cover most eventualities, and VF-143 would undoubtedly have another Tomcat primed and ready should '112's' problem prove unfixable in the short space of time covered by the launches (*Yves Debay*)

Above The familiar emblem of the 'World Famous Pukin' Dogs' of VF-143. Starting life as a winged lion, the legend of the 'Pukin' Dog' originated in Vietnam when a USAF F-105 Thunderchief driver remarked on how unwell the beast looked emblazoned upon the fin of a squadron F-4B. Somehow, VF-143 managed to get official permission to change their nickname and they have been known by this less than tasteful sobriquet ever since. One of the first east coast units to receive the Tomcat, the 'Pukin' Dogs' have flown the F-14 since 1974, the squadron having previously operated the Phantom II since 1963. Interestingly, VF-143 have also been paired with the 'Ghostriders' of VF-142 since 1963, both squadrons completing seven tours of Vietnam with the F-4 between 1964 and 1973 (*Steve Mansfield*)

There are no problems with this 'Pukin' Dog'. The RIO watches the hand signals of the cat crewman squatting down near the second launch track, whilst another green-shirt waits for the shuttle to link in with the towbar strop. The retaining link is already in place behind the nose gear, this vital piece of kit designed to break away from the gear leg as soon as the catapult reaches its full working pressure. Modex '111' is a well used airframe belonging to two separate crew, different names appearing on either side of the canopy rail. Traditionally, naval aviaters fly whatever aircraft happens to be ready for launch, very rarely getting to crew the jet emblazoned with their name on it (*Steve Mansfield*)

With the shuttle and launch bar firmly locked together, and the retaining link ready to take the strain, the crew prepare for afterburner checks before committing themselves for take-off. The crew keep their hands visible in the cockpit whilst the 'deckies' are checking the rear of the aircraft, this simple, but effective, signal allowing the cat officer to send his men in under the Tomcat without having to worry about the pilot or RIO accidentally sweeping the wings or angling the tailplane, both actions capable of having a severely detrimental effect on a young sailors health. As a variation on a standard theme, the armourers have fitted an AIM-7F Sparrow beneath the fuselage in place of the more typical AIM-54 Phoenix. Modex '102' is usually reserved for the XO's Tomcat, as denoted on the canopy rail of this F-14A (*Yves Debay*)

Previous pages With the catapult at full power and the afterburners kicked in, '102' screams down the deck at the start of yet another sortie during *Dragon Hammer '88*. Although rather faded and blotchy, the demarcation line between the grey on the fuselage spine and the lighter shade on the rest of the Tomcat is still clearly visible. This scheme makes for an interesting comparison with that worn by F-14s from VF-41 and -84 (*Yves Debay*)

Above Now this is what separates the men from the boys! Almost free of the carrier deck, a blotchy F-14A shoots away from '*Ike*' off the waist catapult. Still accelerating due to the massive kick of the catapult, the progress of the Tomcat from here on in is down to the screeching TF30s buried in the fuselage of the aircraft. A compressor stall or engine flame-out at this point would force the crew to 'take to the silk', arriving back aboard the carrier courtesy of a Sea King from HS-15! (*Yves Debay*)

Right Keeping the throttles firmly locked in phase five afterburner, the pilot begins to peel away from the carrier. He has already trimmed up the stabilizers, and will soon retract the gear and retard the throttles back to military power, thus reducing the engine's voracious appetite for JP4 (*Yves Debay*)

F-14 Tomcat

Right Once they have attained operational altitude this is what the fighter boys of CVW-7 get up to, amongst other things! This interesting formation comprises four distinctively marked F-14As, three of which show some semblance of former squadron colours. Led by the distinctively painted CAG-ship of VF-143, this quartet of fighters are cruising at height over the Med. As with VF-142, the brightly coloured F-14s of VF-143 disappeared with the advent of the A+(Plus) (*US Navy via Angelo Romano*)

Overleaf 'And break.' The pilot of '104' performs a text book pitch out after the formation clears the carrier, vortices streaming over the wings as the aircraft is reefed into a four G recovery turn. Seconds after '104' has broken formation the remaining pair will follow suit at preset intervals. Each pilot will then sweep the wings of his aircraft forward and lower the undercarriage and tailhook in preparation for landing back aboard the '*Ike*' (*Yves Debay*)

Inset overleaf Just as a good landing back at base is a matter of pride for Air Force pilots, the correct manners in the airspace above a carrier are vitally important for a naval aviator also. With their supersonic glove vanes deployed, a trio of grubby VF-143 Tomcats return to the '*Ike*' after a BARCAP during *Dragon Hammer '88*. The tightness of the formation, and the steadiness maintained by each aircraft, is a sign of skilful flying. To top it all off, the 'Pukin' Dogs' have managed to get three Tomcats airborne with consecutive Modexs! (*Yves Debay*)

Previous pages VF-143's CAG-ship looks good for a three-wire trap back aboard '*Ike*'. As with many squadrons, the 'Dogs' have even customized the external tanks on their CAG aircraft. Deployed between the twin fins is the massive airbrake, this paddle-like device sitting flush behind the beaver tail when not in use. Along with modex '100', VF-143 followed current Navy style by respraying the CO's aircraft in high-viz colours, although the complete scheme of blue with white striping did not appear on '101' until well after the CAG Tomcat had been resprayed (*Yves Debay*)

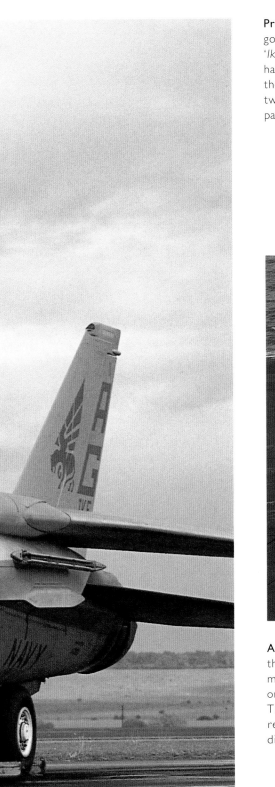

Above With the wire still firmly snagged in the striped tailhook, the CAG Tomcat sits motionless after coming to a dramatic stop on the warm steel deck of the *Eisenhower*. The pilot will soon lower the hook to release the wire, a deck marshaller then directing him forward to a temporary parking spot on the bow of the ship. Although Tomcat squadrons often adorn the flaps of their F-14s with modexs, the style and size of the numerals on this aircraft are obviously non-regulation (*Yves Debay*)

Left Usually cramped aboard the flightdeck jostling for space with other jets from CVW-7, this F-14A+(Plus) was fortunate enough to spend a (wet) weekend away from the '*Ike*' at the Aeroplane and Armament Experimental Establishment (A&AEE) at Boscombe Down in Hampshire, England, in June 1990. Wearing a solemn scheme typical of VF-143 F-14s, this Tomcat didn't exactly set the world alight, particularly in stormy weather. However, the 'macho' crew of this aircraft proved to be anything but drab, the colourful pair signing autographs and answering questions in front of their jet on both days of the Battle of Britain Airshow (*Tony Holmes*)

Reserves, Reworks and Testers

Like its predecessor, the F-4 Phantom II, the Tomcat has also been pressed into service by other non-sea-going units over the years. More often than not, the roles performed by these squadrons have received little coverage, the Tomcat being inextricably linked to the carrier deck, or the flightlines at Miramar and Oceana.

Hundreds of miles north of 'Fightertown' is the expansive Pacific Missile Test Center (PMTC) at Naval Air Station Point Mugu. Basking in the warm Californian sunshine are more than a dozen F-14s wearing either the distinctive PMTC triangle or the classic 'Playboy bunny' of VX-4 on their twin fins. Having played a crucial part in the testing of various models of the F-14, and the aircraft's compatability with its deadly arsenal of short, medium and long range missiles, PMTC and VX-4 Tomcats have flown thousands of hours in support of fleet operations. A test and evaluation unit, VX-4 was also the first Navy squadron on the Pacific coast to receive the F-14A + (Plus), a number of brand new Tomcats being delivered to Point Mugu for missile development tests in early 1988.

Travelling back down to Miramar, you only have to walk a few hundred yards towards the Hawkeye ramp at the eastern end of the field and before you know it you're in Navy Reserve country. Spread out on the sundrenched pan are 24 drab grey Tomcats, these aircraft looking not unlike the other 200 or so F-14s found at Miramar. However, a closer inspection of the tail fins reveals two rather unusual motifs that are rarely seen on carrier decks. Belonging to VF-301 'Devil's Disciples' and VF-302 'Stallions', the Tomcats provide the air superiority cover for CVWR-30, the Pacific fleet reserve air wing. Staffed by veteran naval aviators who now fly commercial jets for a living, the wealth of experience within both squadrons is unmatched by any fleet unit at 'Fightertown'.

Closer to San Diego city is the traditional home of US naval aviation, NAS North Island. Sited on beautiful Coronado Island, the base is home to various anti-submarine warfare units, the hum of S-3 Vikings and the high-pitch din of SH-60s and SH-3s disturbing the peace throughout the year. However, the roar of TF30s in afterburner regularly crackles across the ramp as the Naval Air Rework Facility (NARF) is sited within the confines of North Island. Charged with the responsibility of overhauling all frontline types in the naval inventory, the NARF technicians see more than their fair share of weary Tomcats in a year, a constant stream of high-time fighters arriving at North Island from Miramar for refurbishment. Stripped down to components, the airframe is thoroughly x-rayed, pressure tested, re-wired and then re-assembled. More often than not, zero-time TF30s are also inserted into the engine bays of the F-14, thus allowing the aircraft to perform as well as it would have a decade or so earlier when it first left Calverton.

F-14 Tomcat

Previous pages The steam from the waist cat drifts upwards through the launch track and obscures the undercarriage of this VF-302 F-14 as it is attached to the shuttle. Sitting in their revetment immediately in front of the Tomcat are the 'shooters', these aptly named sailors having to signal to the engineers below deck to fire the catapult when the deck officer drops to his knee and points to the bow. As with any frontline air wing, CVWR-30 brought their own deck crew personnel aboard the USS *Enterprise* (CVN-65) for their AcDuTra period in August 1988. Prior to the deployment only 20 per cent of the deck personnel were carrier-qualified, but in less than a week all members of CVWR-30's 'roof crew' were fully up to speed with blue water ops (*Frank B Mormillo*)

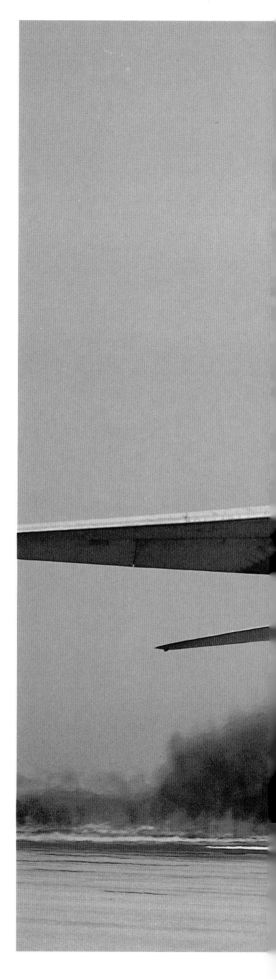

Right Several hundred miles from home, a typically drab 'Stallions' F-14 closes in on the main drag at NAS Point Mugu. As is the case with virtually all reserve Tomcats, this aircraft carries no external tanks, its only store being a single dummy AIM-9 'Mike' secured to the starboard shoulder-pylon. Although not often seen with belly tanks, VF-302 F-14s regularly carry a TARPS pod beneath the fuselage, the squadron fulfilling the reconnaissance duties for CVWR-30. A relatively new unit, VF-302 was the second fighter reserve squadron formed as part of the air wing in May 1971. Always based at Miramar, the 'Stallions' initially flew the F-8K Crusader before becoming the first fully-fledged reserve fighter squadron in the Navy to operate the F-4B Phantom II. Reworked F-4Ns from the North Island NARF replaced the Bravo models in 1975, the squadron getting many hours of use out of the slightly more advanced Phantom IIs. Involved in the confusing aircraft swap of 1981 which saw the fighter elements of CVWR-30 exchange their tired F-4Ns for the 'hot' F-4Ss of CVW-14, VF-302 proceeded to fly the ultimate Navy Phantom II until the first reserve F-14s arrived at Miramar in 1985 (*Frank B Mormillo*)

F-14 Tomcat

Right Fire and steam. Disappearing behind its own heat haze, a colourless F-14A from VF-301 rockets off the bow of the '*Big E*' during the AcDuTra det. During the 11-day cruise both VF-301 and -302 loosed off five AIM-9Hs during a live-fire MissilEx (Missile Exercise) against drone targets. Both units also provided air wing cover during MasEx (Maritime air superiority) missions with other elements of CVWR-30. As with the reservist deck crew, only a quarter of the pilots and RIOs at VF-301 were carrier qualified when the cruise commenced, this figure reaching 100 per cent before the det was completed (*Frank B Mormillo*)

Below Putting the Tomcat through its paces at the Point Mugu open house in October 1983, a PMTC pilot pulls the stick back soon after completing an afterburner departure and zoom climbs away from California. Despite being storeless, this F-14 still has a pair of Phoenix missile pallets firmly bolted to its fuselage, these units containing various interfacing and cooling components for the long range weapon. They also cover the recesses in the fuselage provided for the Sparrow missile. One of the oldest Tomcats still in service today, this aircraft (BuNo 158625) was part of the second production batch of F-14s ordered by the Navy way back in 1971 (*Frank B Mormillo*)

High above southern California, a 'clean' Tomcat cruises along during a routine training sortie out of Miramar. The arrow motif of VF-301 bears a strong resemblance to the design worn on the twin fins of VF-103 'Sluggers' Tomcats, this full-time unit being based at NAS Oceana. Lacking the Northrop AXX-1 Television Camera Set (TCS) beneath the radome (hence the bullet fairing cover), this aircraft does, however, wear the Battle 'E' and Safety 'S' beneath the canopy. As with VF-302, the 'Devil's Disciples' received some of the oldest F-14s in fleet service as replacements for their F-4s in 1984. Two other reserve units currently operate the Tomcat; VF-201 'Rangers' and VF-202 'Superheats', both squadrons flying from NAS Dallas, Texas, in support of the east coast reserve wing, CVWR-20 (*Frank B Mormillo*)

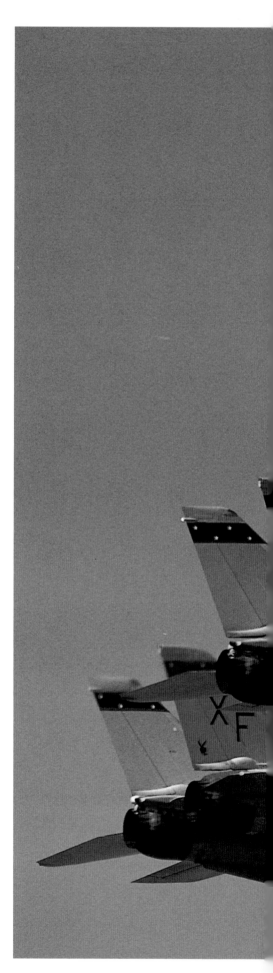

Above Safely plugged in and green light aglow, a VX-4 F-14 gets its tanks topped up during the Point Mugu open house in 1986. Providing the fuel for the VX-4 Tomcat on this occasion is a veteran KA-3B Skywarrior from Point Mugu-based VAQ-34 'Electric Horsemen'. Commissioned at Mugu in September 1952, VX-4 performed much of the pioneering work on early air-to-air missiles throughout the fifties and into the early sixties, utilizing a varied fleet of aircraft ranging from the F-3D Skynight through to the venerable F-4 Phantom II. An early recipient of the F-14, VX-4 have had up to a dozen Tomcats on strength at various times since late 1972. For many years only the standard A-model was to be found at Point Mugu, but since early 1988 several A+(Plus) Tomcats have also featured on the squadron books (*Frank B Mormillo*)

Right Slightly younger than their PMTC ramp mate, this pair of VX-4 'Evaluators' F-14s aren't spring chickens either, having both been delivered in the mid 1970s. Still wearing full unit colours when this photo was taken in November 1981, the Tomcats of VX-4 have since been toned down in accordance with current Navy doctrine. Both aircraft carry the small ALQ-100 ECM antennae fairing beneath their radomes, with the formation leader also having an infrared seeker squeezed in between the nose and the ECM blister on his F-14 (*Frank B Mormillo*)

Left Wearing a scheme more appropriate for jungle warfare, a recently refurbished Tomcat undergoes engine power checks at the NARF complex at North Island. The aircraft is covered in zinc chromate primer yellow, this rather disgusting colour being ideal as a base for the low-viz greys which the aircraft will eventually leave the NARF wearing. Firmly chained to restraining blocks cemented in the ramp, the F-14 is having its twin TF30s thoroughly checked in all power settings from idle through to full phase five afterburner. Just as you would find with a frontline Tomcat, this F-14 has all the rescue stencils and ejection seat warning traingles sprayed onto it (*John Dibbs*)

Overleaf Identified only as 'G611', the Tomcat is attached to various external generators and metering systems. Several spine panels have been left off this aircraft to allow the civilian technicians access to the electrical and control system ducting and the tailplane and fin connecting rods. Mobile FOD (foreign object debris) guards are also securely fitted over both intakes. Only after exhaustive ground runs is the aircraft permitted to fly, an experienced NARF test crew taking the 'reborn' Grumman fighter aloft for airborne checks. Older F-14As are currently being updated at Calverton with the installation of F110s and various systems upgrades, finished airframes being redesignated as F-14A+(Plus) models (*Both photos by John Dibbs*)